Normal Norma

Joanna Nadin

Illustrated by
Joe Todd-Stanton

OXFORD
UNIVERSITY PRESS

OXFORD
UNIVERSITY PRESS

Great Clarendon Street, Oxford, OX2 6DP,
United Kingdom

Oxford University Press is a department of the University of Oxford.
It furthers the University's objective of excellence in research, scholarship,
and education by publishing worldwide. Oxford is a registered trade mark of
Oxford University Press in the UK and in certain other countries

Text © Joanna Nadin 2017

Illustrations © Joe Todd-Stanton 2017

The moral rights of the author have been asserted

First published 2017

British Library Cataloguing in Publication Data
Data available

978-0-19-837770-2

1 3 5 7 9 10 8 6 4 2

Paper used in the production of this book is a natural, recyclable product
made from wood grown in sustainable forests. The manufacturing process
conforms to the environmental regulations of the country of origin.

Printed in China by Leo Paper Products Ltd.

Acknowledgements
Inside cover notes written by Gill Howell
Author photograph by Helen Giles

Contents

Chapter 1
Normal Norma

Norma was normal. Everything about her was normal. Her house was normal, her family was normal and, despite his name, even her dog Captain Fabulous was normal. All boringly, snoringly normal.

And Norma hated it.

What she wanted was a life like the ones she read about in books. She wanted to fight dragons in far-off lands. She wanted to defeat a troll with her knowledge of riddles. She had learned seventy-three riddles just in case, but so far no troll had even bothered to show up.

Most of all, she wanted to find a way into another world at the back of someone's wardrobe. She kept looking, but so far all she'd found was an odd sock, a chocolate raisin and four pairs of flip-flops, none of which fitted.

But still, Norma kept hoping. Maybe an alien would land in her back garden. Maybe giants would take over the town. Maybe Captain Fabulous would turn out to be the world's first talking dog …

"Go on," Norma said to Captain Fabulous. "Say something! Tell me a joke!" But Captain Fabulous didn't tell a joke, or say anything at all. He just went on licking a shoe.

"It's not fair," Norma said. "In books, dogs can talk. In books, anything can happen! I could have a ... a magic parrot instead. Or a dragon!"

"You should be glad that those kinds of shenanigans do only happen in books," warned Mum. "Imagine the mess if we really did have a pet dragon."

"I wouldn't mind," muttered Norma. "I wouldn't mind at all." And she stomped off out to see her friend Manjit.

"What room can no one enter?" Norma asked as they sat on the wall outside Manjit's house.

"I don't know," said Manjit. "One with a locked door?"

Norma sighed. "No, it's a riddle. Think harder."

Manjit thought harder but he couldn't solve the puzzle, so Norma

told him the answer.

"It's a *mush*room!" Norma said triumphantly. "Do you get it?"

But Manjit didn't get it. "You can't go into a mushroom," he said.

Norma shook her head. "You'd be hopeless if a troll turned up."

Manjit shrugged his shoulders, because he knew full well that a troll wasn't going to turn up on Preston Street anytime soon. "Want a go on my scooter?" he asked instead.

"Is it a Spy Scooter with an invisibility shield, a super-stun button and a thing that plays a theme tune?" asked Norma.

"Er, no," said Manjit, a bit nonplussed. "It's just a scooter. But it does make a weird noise when you go really fast."

"No thanks, then," said Norma. "Maybe tomorrow."

But there were other plans in store for tomorrow. Big plans. And Norma was about to find out what.

Chapter 2
The Sleepover

The next morning, Norma and Captain
Fabulous sat in the kitchen. Norma was
at the table eating toast, and Captain
Fabulous was on the floor eating the
bits Norma dropped when Mum wasn't
looking. It was the first day of the
holidays and Norma's head was full of
thoughts about the exciting things that
might happen …

Maybe a chief spy would telephone, asking her to take part in a top secret mission to save a kidnapped prince.

Maybe she would find buried treasure in the park and be rewarded with a medal and her own TV show.

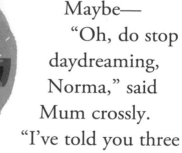

Maybe—

"Oh, do stop daydreaming, Norma," said Mum crossly.

"I've told you three times we're leaving for Granny's in half an hour and you still haven't packed your suitcase."

"Pardon?" said Norma, who had only heard the word 'suitcase'. She was hoping they were off to the jungle to track a legendary beast or two.

Mum sighed. "I said, we're off to Granny's."

"Granny's?" It was Norma's turn to sigh. "But why?"

"Because I'm going away for a work thing," Mum said. "So Granny's looking after you. I did tell you yesterday before you went to bed."

But yesterday before bed, Norma had been fighting an imaginary bear with only her wit and her bare hands, and she hadn't had time to listen to Mum.

"Is it because you've got to go and catch a criminal?" she asked hopefully. "The Great Sophistico? Or Morangatang, the world's most villainous monkey?"

"I work in a bank, Norma," said Mum. "You know that. And there is no 'Great' anything, and definitely no villainous monkeys."

Norma did know that, but she also knew that spies always pretended to work in banks. She was hoping that, secretly, Mum was going to fly off in a helicopter to a foreign land, wearing a magnificent disguise.

"Whatever it is you're thinking right now, you can think again," said Mum. "I'm going to be looking at flip charts with Boring Bob and that's that. Now chip-chop and get packing."

Norma slid down from her chair with a sulky look on her face. Granny's house indeed. It would be all right if her granny was anything like the ones in books. In books, grannies were mysterious and got up to all sorts of shenanigans. But Norma's Granny was small and grey and granny-like, and she didn't get up to anything except eating biscuits and playing bingo with Maurice next door.

Worst of all, she had a cat. A fat,
black, cantankerous cat called Dave
who hated all dogs, especially Captain
Fabulous. That meant Captain Fabulous
would have to stay with Mrs Beasley
over the road. Captain Fabulous didn't
mind so much because Mrs Beasley
fed him sandwiches and let him watch
television. But Norma minded. Norma
minded a lot, and as she packed her
clean pants, her socks and her storybook
into her suitcase, she huffed and puffed
and grumbled.

"Cheer up," said Mum, as she heaved Norma's case into the car. "You never know, something amazing might happen."

But Norma did know. She knew that at Granny's house absolutely nothing amazing would happen. Unless you counted a game of cards and a slice of fruit cake as amazing. Which Norma didn't. In fact, the chances of anything remotely interesting happening at Granny's were about as likely as a flying snowman showing up in the back garden. And that wasn't very likely at all, as even Norma knew. After all, she'd been looking out for flying snowmen every morning for the last year and a half, and so far she hadn't seen a single one.

Chapter 3
Granny's House

"You know, Granny's moved house," said Mum as they drove into Chipping Bigbury.

Norma, who had been staring out of the window checking for pirates or Vikings, turned around. "Moved?" she asked, her eyes lighting up. Maybe she'd been wrong – maybe something amazing could happen after all! Perhaps Granny had moved to a massive mansion, or a ruined castle, or an underground lair with a shark pool and a lot of machines that went 'ding'.

"Yes, you'll see," said Mum. "It's a smashing place."

But when the car pulled to a halt outside Granny's house, Norma's eyes unlit and her heart sank again. Number 22 Arkwright Avenue wasn't a mansion or a castle or an underground lair. It was a bungalow. Whoever heard of brilliant adventures happening in a bungalow? Why, bungalows didn't even have attics or cellars to hide treasure or escaped black mambas in. Norma climbed out of the car and trudged to the front door with yet another massive sigh.

Mum knew exactly what Norma was thinking. "It'll be far more interesting inside, you'll see."

But it wasn't, not as far as Norma was concerned.

"Ooh, Norma, isn't this exciting!"
exclaimed Granny after Mum had gone.
"What shall we do first? The world is
our lobster! Or at least the bungalow
is. I'd stay out of the back garden at
the moment though because it's a right
forest. I need to get Maurice around to
do some weeding."

Norma eyed Dave the cat, who eyed
Norma right back.

"Tell you what," continued Granny.
"Why don't you go off and explore
while I pop the kettle on? I might even
be able to find a biscuit or two."

Norma cheered slightly at the thought of a biscuit or two (or three) and slid off the sofa to look around the bungalow. Maybe there would be something strange or dangerous hidden here after all – a dinosaur egg hatching under the bed, perhaps. Or a cowgirl hiding out in the wardrobe. Or, best of all, a secret passageway to a special land …

But in the wardrobe, Norma could only find old coats and cardigans.

Under the bed, she could only find a crumpled-up toffee wrapper and a pair of pink, furry slippers.

Norma checked everywhere but there was no secret passageway anywhere, as far as she could see. The bedrooms just had beds, the bathroom was just a bathroom, and the hallway was nothing more than a long corridor with pictures of cats on the walls and a cupboard with a very stiff handle.

"What's in there?" asked Norma, rattling it.

"Oh, just old junk," said Granny. "Oojamaflips and thingamabobs and whatnots. I wouldn't bother if I were you. Besides, Dave will only wander in and get stuck inside."

"What are oojamaflips?" asked Norma.

"Paint tins, mainly. And the odd broken clock or two," said Granny.

Norma sighed. It was hopeless. Nothing exciting was going to happen, and that was that.

"Don't look so glum," said Granny. "How about a nice chocolate biscuit and a game of cards?"

"I'd rather play riddles," said Norma.

"Then riddles it is," said Granny. "It'll be fun. You'll see."

And it *was* fun, sort of. By bedtime, Norma had baffled Granny with nineteen riddles, won eight games of cards and eaten two slices of cherry cake. But she was still disappointed.

"Never mind," said Granny as she tucked Norma in. "I'm sure your dreams will be full of adventure."

"I hope so," said Norma. "I want a forest and a castle and a battle with a giant."

"Oh, you are funny," said Granny. "Night, Norma."

"Night, Granny," said Norma, and she hoped with all her heart that Granny was right. At least she could dream an excellent adventure.

Chapter 4
The Oojamaflip
Cupboard

Granny was right. That night, Norma
dreamed an excellent dream about a
talking cat called The Colonel who took
her on a wild adventure in the land
of fairytales, where giants roamed and
wolves hid in the woods. She was just
getting to the rickety bridge where the
troll lived, when something woke her up.

"Oh bother," said Norma to herself,
and she pulled the duvet higher above
her head.

But the thing that had woken her clanked again, and this time Norma sat up in bed. "Granny?" she whispered. But Granny was fast asleep next door and snoring louder than a cow with a cold.

"I suppose I shall have to investigate," said Norma. "In case it's burglars. Or a unicorn." And she hopped out of bed and out the door.

The noise was coming from the cupboard in the hallway. "But there's nothing in there but oojamaflips," sighed Norma. "And thingamabobs and whatnots. Unless …" She remembered what Granny had said about the cat getting trapped.

"Dave?" she whispered, and turned the handle. The door was stiff but she pulled and pulled, and eventually it flew open. Norma walked inside.

The cupboard was bigger than she had imagined, but Granny had been telling the truth. It was packed to the ceiling with oojamaflips and thingamabobs and whatnots, all stacked willy-nilly on the shelves. But there was something else too: something scratching towards the back of the cupboard, near a teetering pile of paint tins, saucepans and dusty old clocks. Norma peered into the gloom and shuffled a bit further forward. "Come on," she called. "Come to Norma."

But Dave didn't come.

"Oh really," she said crossly. "This is ruining my good dream. I might just leave you in here if you're going to be so difficult." And she stamped her foot ready to give Dave a piece of her mind. But as she did so, she wobbled in the darkness and knocked right into the tower of oojamaflips. She sent them teetering and tottering and tipping, until one of them tipped right off the edge and on to Norma's head … at which point everything went black.

When Norma opened her eyes
a moment later she was still in the
cupboard, but now she had a lump on
her head and a silver teapot in her lap.

"Oh," she said. "It looks almost like
a genie lamp." And, even though she
was pretty sure it was nothing more than
a teapot, she gave it a rub. She wished
that Manjit would make the National
Scooter Squad, because he had been
going on about it for months. But then
she had another thought.

"What if it is a magic lamp?" she wondered. "I won't know if it works until I see Manjit in the morning. I'd better make another wish, just in case." And she did. She wished that there was another world just waiting to be explored at the back of the cupboard – a world with giants and trolls and wolves, and possibly a magnificent castle with a massive tea laid on just for her. Then she rubbed the lamp and waited.

And waited.

And waited.

She was just about to give up and go back to bed when something interrupted her.

"What is it we're waiting for, exactly?" said the voice.

"Huh?" asked Norma, jumping, then looking wildly around her. "It can't be," she thought to herself. "Can it?" Because there, at the very back of the cupboard, was a cat.

"Dave?" asked Norma.
"The Colonel, actually," said the cat.

At that name, Norma felt her tummy jump. "And where, exactly, are we, er, Colonel?" asked Norma.

"How should I know?" asked The Colonel. "I'm a cat. But I can tell you there are some awfully strange and dangerous things that way." And he nodded to the back of the cupboard, where a pale light now glimmered.

"Really?" asked Norma, her eyes popping with the thought of it.

"Really," said The Colonel. "Though I'd rather we just went back to Granny's house. I'm awfully peckish and rather fancy a sardine sandwich."

"Granny's house?" asked Norma. "Granny's house? Not on your nelly. I've been waiting for an adventure forever, and I'm not going back for anything, especially not sardines. Yuk."

"Oh," said The Colonel wearily. "Then I suppose I shall have to accompany you."

"I suppose you shall!" said Norma.
And with a spring in her step and what
felt like magic beans in her tummy,
Norma set off towards the light, with
The Colonel sighing loudly behind her.

Chapter 5
The Troll

The World On The Other Side Of The Cupboard was exactly as Norma had dreamed. There was a wild and wonderful forest, a big beanstalk that disappeared up into the clouds where only a giant could possibly live, and a very promising castle. One that looked as if it would have jam tarts and cream cakes, and even sardine sandwiches for The Colonel.

Best of all, just a few steps in front of them, was a rickety bridge.

"Brilliant!" said Norma. "Riddle time!"

"I think you'll find …" began The Colonel.

But Norma wasn't listening. Instead she marched straight on to the bridge, trying very hard to make a trip-trap sound with her feet.

"Halt!" came a voice. "Who goes there?"

Norma's face lit up. "It's Norma!" she said. "I've come to play riddles."

"Oooh!" came the voice from under the bridge. "I like a riddle." And with that, out popped a short man in an enormous hat.

"A troll!" said Norma.

"Mr Miggins, actually," said the man. "But you can call me whatever you like if you can answer me this: what word becomes shorter when you add two letters to it?"

Norma hadn't heard this riddle before and had to think.

"Do you know? Do you know?" asked Mr Miggins, hopping up and down. "I'll tell you, shall I? It's 'short'. Get it? 'Short' becomes 'shorter' when you add two letters."

"Well, I might have got it if you'd given me a chance," said Norma crossly. "Do another one."

"All right," said Mr Miggins. "What can you catch but not throw?"

But before Norma could ponder the answer, Mr Miggins blurted it out. "It's a cold!" he said. "Clever, isn't it! How about this one: what weighs more, a kilo of feathers or a kilo of bricks? It's neither! They both weigh a kilo."

Norma stuck her hands on her hips. "This is ridiculous," she announced.

"How is this a game if you keep
giving away the answers? Come along,
Colonel." And she stomped straight
past Mr Miggins to the other side of
the bridge. "And by the way, you were
supposed to stop me then," she called
over her shoulder. "Honestly, what kind
of troll are you?"

"I don't think that's very kind,"
said The Colonel.

"Well, he wasn't doing what trolls
are supposed to do," replied Norma.
"Everyone who's read a book knows
that. Trolls are supposed to stop you
if you don't know the answer to
the riddle."

"Life isn't always like it is in books,"
warned The Colonel.

"More's the pity," said Norma.

"Where to now, then?" asked The
Colonel.

Norma eyed The World On The
Other Side Of The Cupboard. "Straight
through the enchanted forest, up the
beanstalk to get the golden goose, then
to the castle for tea."

"Sounds simple," said The Colonel.

But it wasn't. It wasn't simple at all.

Chapter 6
The Wolf, the Beanstalk and the Horrible Giant

For starters, an enormous wolf leaped into their path.

"Hello," he said, his teeth glinting. "Are you off to Granny's house? Oh, do say you are. I've always wanted to meet Granny!"

Norma rolled her eyes. "No, we're not and no, you can't. We've just come from Granny's house and we're not going back for hours."

"That's a shame," said the wolf, making a sad face. "That way, is it?" And he pointed down the path they'd come from.

"Yes. Only I wouldn't bother if I were you. It's boring back there."

"Norma," said The Colonel. "Don't you think …"

But Norma didn't think at all. She was too busy eyeing the beanstalk. "Right," she said. "Up I go. Are you coming, Colonel?"

"No, I really don't think …"

But again, Norma ignored the cat and his thinking, and began to climb. One foot above the other, she made her way up the leaves, just as she'd read about in books.

"Halloooo," she called up the stalk.

"Halloooo, giant. I'm coming to get you!" Then she called down to The Colonel. "It's brilliant up here. I can see for miles. I can see the castle, I can see the cupboard door, I can even see the wolf!"

"Norma," said The Colonel calmly. "About that wolf …"

"I know," said Norma. "Wasn't he brilliant? Just like in the story. You know, when he goes to Granny's house and eats her up and …"

"… Yes?" asked The Colonel.

"Oh dear," said Norma.

"Oh dear indeed," said The Colonel. "You told him exactly where Granny lives and that we wouldn't be back for hours."

"Oops?" said Norma.

"I'd say it was more than 'oops'," said The Colonel. "I'd say it was more of a disaster. Or a tragedy. Or a calamity. Or a ..."

"OK, OK, I get the picture," said Norma. "I'd better come down."

"Yes, I think you'd better," said The Colonel.

"So do I," said a thunderous voice from above.

The Colonel looked up.

Norma looked up.

There, halfway down the beanstalk, was an enormous man with enormous hands and enormous feet, and an enormous scowl on his face.

"Are you …" began Norma.

" … a giant?" finished The Colonel.

The giant smiled a nasty smile. "Fee, fi, fo, fum," he said. "I smell the blood of a cat and a small girl who've just woken me up from my nap."

"That's not how it goes," said Norma.

"Are you really going to wait around to argue over a rhyme, or are you going to scram?" asked The Colonel.

Norma thought for a moment. "Scram," she said decisively.

"Good," said The Colonel. "Then let's go."

Chapter 7
The Race

"Run!" cried Norma, her feet flying down the path.

"I am!" called The Colonel. "Honestly, if you'd just listened to me in the first place …"

"How was I to know the wolf would try to get Granny? Or that the giant would come after me?"

"Well, you're the one who's read all the stories," the cat pointed out.

Norma kept quiet after that because it was true: she should have known this would happen. She'd even wanted it to happen. Except now that it was happening, she found she didn't really like it at all.

"Fee, fi, fo, fum," came the thunderous voice of the giant behind them.

"He's getting closer," said The Colonel.

"I know that, clever clogs," said
Norma. "But look, the bridge!"

And sure enough, in front of them
was the rickety bridge, and on top of it
sat Mr Miggins with his arms and legs
crossed, and a cross look on his face.

"Halt," he said. "Who goes there?"

"It's me," said Norma.

"Who's 'me'?" asked Mr Miggins, meanly.

Norma could feel her tummy tighten with annoyance and worry. "Norma," she said quickly. "It's Norma. Remember? You told me riddles earlier. And gave me all the answers."

"Oh yes," snapped Mr Miggins. "How could I forget?"

"So can we go across?" Norma asked impatiently. "Only there's a giant after us."

Mr Miggins thought. "Very well," he said. "But first you must answer me this: what goes up a chimney down, but can't go down a chimney up?"

"Seriously?" asked Norma. "Now you want to play?"

"What's the answer?" Mr Miggins said, ignoring her. "Tell me or you can't cross."

Norma thought. And she thought. And she thought. But she couldn't think of the answer.

"I ..."

"You don't know," laughed Mr Miggins. "Ha! I win, I win!"

"Fine," said Norma. "You win. Now tell me what it is and then let us through."

"Shan't," said Mr Miggins.

Norma felt the ground begin to shake with the thud of enormous footsteps. "Fee, fi, fo, fum," came the call, closer and closer.

"Please!" she begged.

But still Mr Miggins refused to budge.

"If only we had three wishes," sighed The Colonel. "Then we could just magic ourselves away."

"If only," agreed Norma. "But that sort of nonsense only happens in books … Oh, hang on." Norma reached into her pocket and pulled out the silver teapot that had fallen on to her head in the oojamaflip cupboard.

"Well, well, well," said The Colonel. "How splendid."

"You can't use that," said Mr Miggins angrily. "That's cheating!"

"Watch me," said Norma.

Then Norma wished harder than

she'd ever done for anything in her life. "I wish to go back to Granny's," she said. "And I wish for everything to be normal again. Nice and safe and normal." Then she closed her eyes and rubbed the lamp, and hoped with all her heart.

Chapter 8
Back at Granny's House

Norma opened her eyes. No giant.
No beanstalk. No Mr Miggins on a
rickety bridge. She sighed with relief.
The World On The Other Side Of The
Cupboard was right where it belonged,
and she was back where she belonged: in
bed at Granny's house.

Then Norma remembered something, or rather, someone. Someone with a horribly hairy face, someone with big, glinting teeth, someone who'd been heading to Granny's house himself the last time she'd seen him …

"The wolf!" she cried. "Oh no!" She leaped out of bed and scooted next door to Granny's bedroom.

There in bed, still fast asleep, and still snoring louder than a cow with a cold, lay Granny.

Or at least, it looked like Granny. "Only, what if the wolf really had eaten her up and disguised himself as an old lady?" thought Norma. "And what if he were about to eat me too?"

Norma tugged carefully at the duvet. "Granny?" she whispered.

Granny didn't wake up.

Norma crept closer and poked at the bed with a fly swatter. "Granny?" she said, louder this time.

Granny didn't wake up.

Norma crept closer still, until she could feel Granny's breath on her face and see the hairs up Granny's nose. "Granny!" she shouted.

Granny's eyes snapped open. Then her mouth fell open. Then she let out a yell. "Norma Harriet Jones! What on *earth* are you doing?"

"I-I was just checking you're not a wolf!" replied Norma. "You can't be too careful."

"You jolly well can be too careful," said Granny. "I was just dreaming about meringues and you woke me up. Honestly, you and your imagination."

"It's not imagination," said Norma.

"Oh really?" said Granny. "Next you'll be telling me there's a troll in my oojamaflip cupboard."

"There is," said Norma.

Granny laughed. "And I suppose Dave here can talk, can he?" And she stroked the cat who lay on the bed eyeing Norma quietly and sullenly.

"He *can* talk," thought Norma. "And he's not called Dave, he's called The Colonel." But she didn't say anything, because she knew Granny wouldn't believe her. Why, she wasn't even sure if she believed herself any more. I mean, who ever heard of another world at the back of a cupboard, with a wolf and a beanstalk and a troll who told riddles? Not in real life anyway.

And just as well.

"So what do you want to do this morning?" asked Granny. "Hunt for pirates? Dig for treasure? Look for foxes in the walls? Or, we could even tidy up the oojamaflip cupboard if you fancy it."

Norma thought. And thought.
And thought.

"How about a quiet game of cards,"
she said. "And maybe a riddle or two."

"Splendid," said Granny. "That
sounds exciting, doesn't it?"

"It does," said Norma. And the thing
was, it really did.

"I've got a good one," said Norma, after she'd won her eighth game of cards and eaten her third biscuit. "What goes up a chimney down, but can't go down a chimney up?"

"Oh, that's easy," said Granny. "An umbrella." And with that she gave Norma a big wink.

Chapter 9
Nice and Normal

"How was Granny's house?" asked Mum as she and Norma walked back through their own front door, Captain Fabulous trotting happily behind. "Anything exciting happen?"

"Nothing much," said Norma. "We just stayed in and played card games, mainly."

"That sounds nice," said Mum.

"It was," admitted Norma.

"No secret passageway then?" Mum asked.

Norma snorted. "Don't be daft," she said. "They're only in books. And so are giants and magic lamps and wolves that eat grandmothers."

Mum smiled. "If you say so, Norma."

"I do," said Norma. "Now can I go around Manjit's? I might try his scooter today after all."

"Of course," said Mum. "But no
talking to trolls on the way."

Norma rolled her eyes, and stomped
off to Manjit's.

But when she got to Manjit's house,
he wasn't there.

"The strangest thing happened," said Manjit's dad. "A man rang yesterday asking Manjit if he'd like to join the National Scooter Squad."

Norma felt her tummy swirl. "Really?"

"Really," said Manjit's dad. "He's there at the moment, doing some training. They think he's got world champion potential. Imagine that."

"Imagine," agreed Norma, turning pale. "Just imagine …"

About the author

When I was your age, I didn't want to be a writer, I wanted to be *in* a book. Life seemed so much more interesting on the pages than in the small town I lived in. So, when I went to stay at my granny's house, I spent lots of time looking for treasure and secret passageways at the back of cupboards and inside wardrobes.

I never found anything – just oojamaflips and thingamabobs. And none of the jobs I did when I was older were exciting enough either, so in the end I decided to write some adventures of my own – usually about small children with very big imaginations, just like me.